The Productive Mom

Penny White

Published by Penny White, 2023.

While every precaution has been taken in the preparation of this book, the publisher assumes no responsibility for errors or omissions, or for damages resulting from the use of the information contained herein.

THE PRODUCTIVE MOM

First edition. December 2, 2023.

Copyright © 2023 Penny White.

ISBN: 979-8223803218

Written by Penny White.

Table of Contents

I express my gratitude to my Mother for imparting the value of strength and resilience, allowing me to overcome moments of doubt and emerge as the mother I am today. Your absence is deeply felt. My heartfelt appreciation goes to Aunt Debbie for her unwavering support during my times of need. I extend my sincere thanks to my sons, Zachary and Zane, for their belief in me, which inspired and empowered me to complete this book.

THE PRODUCTIVE MOM

First edition. December 2, 2023.

ISBN: 979-8223803218 Written by Penny White.

I would like to think my Mother for teaching me how to be strong and

helping me become the Mother I am today. You are truly missed. And to my

Aunt Debbie,think you for always be- ing there for me when I needed you the most. And to my kids if it was not for you this book would not been written. Thank you for believing in your Mom when everyone else didn't.

TABLE OF CONTENTS

THE PRODUCTIVE MOM

Becoming a productive mom is a multifac- eted journey that requires a blend of orga- niza- tion, time manage- ment, and self-care.

As a mother, the role extends far beyond caretaker to in- clude orchestrating a harmo- nious balance between fami- ly, personal aspirations, and daily responsibilities. This

introduction aims to provide

insights and practical tips for mothers seeking to enhance their productivity while nurturing a thriving household.

Embracing Time Management:
Efficient time management is the corner- stone of productivity for moms. Creating a re- alistic daily schedule that accommodates both family and person- al obligations is crucial. Prior- itizing tasks based on urgency and importance allows for a more focused ap- proach to daily responsibilities.

Setting Realistic Goals:
Understanding personal limits and setting achievable goals is key to maintaining productivity without overwhelming oneself. Whether it's com- pleting household chores, pursuing a career, or engag- ing in personal hobbies, establishing realistic expecta- tions fosters a sense of ac- complishment and reduces stress. **Effective Communication:**

Clear communication within the family is vital. Sharing responsibilities with a partner or involv- ing children in age-appropriate tasks fos- ters a col- laborative atmosphere. Open commu- nication en- sures that everyone is on the same page regarding dai- ly schedules, expectations, and potential challenges.

Self-Care as a Priority:
Productivity is closely tied to personal well- being.
Moms often find themselves neglecting self-care,
but recognizing its importance is es- sential. Taking
time for self-reflection, pursuing hobbies, and ensuring adequate rest are vital components of maintaining mental and physical
hea lth .
Utilizing Technology and Tools:
In the digital age, various tools and apps can assist
moms in managing their time effectively. From calendar apps to meal planning tools, technologycan-
beavaluableallyinstreamlining tasks and reducing
mental load.
Flexibility and Adaptability:
Flexibility is a cornerstone of successful motherhood.

Unexpected challenges are in- evitable, and
being adaptable allows moms to navigate
unforeseen circumstances without sac- ri-
ficing productivity.

Embracing change with a positive mindset fosters resilience.

Building a Support Network:

No mom can do it all alone. Building a strong support network, whether through friends, family, or online communities, provides an invaluable resource for advice, assistance, and emotional support. Surrounding oneself with like-minded individuals can create a sense of camaraderie and shared experiences.

In conclusion, being a productive mom in- volves a holistic approach that encompasses ef- fective time management, realistic goal-setting, open communication, self-care, technology uti- liza- tion, flexibility, and a strong support net- work. By integrating these elements into daily life, mothers can not only manage their respon- sibilities more efficiently but also cultivate a ful- filling and balanced family life.

You CAN Be Productive and Organized!

Do you ever feel like your life is going by too quickly? Are you constantly trying to pick up the pieces and you just don't know how to keep up? You get the dishes cleaned but you look around the house and everything else is a disaster. You forget about important events or homework assignments for the kids. You just *can't seem to get ahead.*

If this sounds like something you're dealing with, this book will give you the tools you need to lower your stress and get the job done.

In this book, we'll help you discover ways to organize your home and become more productive.

These steps are not painful, and they won't take up all your time. They're paths to success that nearly every person can do, and they won't leave you feeling tired and exhausted at the end of the day.

Decluttering the Home

With its rise in popularity, you've probably heard the word "minimalism" before. You either *love* it or it makes you want to run and hide.

You don't want to give up all your precious belongings!

Don't worry. **You don't have to live a spartan life in order to be organized.** But decluttering *is* a really good way to start the process of organization. Here's how you can do it without getting rid of the things you love.

Why is Decluttering Important?

Here are some really good reasons to start your organizational process by decluttering your home:

- Clutter makes you feel claustrophobic. It can make it feel like the room is caving in on you.
- It's been proven—clutter causes stress.
- It's easier to stay organized when you know what you have.
- Once you declutter, you'll have more space to work with.
- It's easier to clean when you have fewer belongings.
- You'll have more time to do what you love when you have fewer things to worry about.
- Fewer things mean you have less to dust—

who has time to dust every little knickknack?

How Do You Start Decluttering Your Home?

How do you eat an elephant? One bite at a time.

The same is true for decluttering your house. If you try to take on the whole house at once, you'll likely feel overwhelmed. Chances are you'll quit before you make much progress.

You may be in the spirit to kick out all your rubbish but **take it one room at a time.**

Try choosing common areas that you use often. Popular places to start are your kitchen or living room. Because you spend so much time there, you'll be reminded each day of how good it felt to declutter that space. Your new decluttered space will feel totally refreshed.

What Do You Keep, What Do You Toss?

Let's say you start by decluttering your kitchen. How do you know which items to keep, which to donate, and which to throw away?

A lot of organizational gurus suggest going through your items one by one. Ask yourself these questions:

- Do I use this item? ● Do I like this item?
- How often do I use it?
- When was the last time I used it?
- Do I already have four of the same thing?
- Do I need that many?

THE PRODUCTIVE MOM -

Am I only keeping this because someone

●

gave it to me?
Can I replace this item with something

●

smaller?
I didn't remember I owned this item, but

●

I love it. How do I fit it into my life?

Your answers to these questions will help guide your decisions. Often, once you start going through your belongings, you'll find things that you don't like, don't need, or have multiples of.

As a general rule, if something is broken and can't be repaired (or would be costly to repair) toss it. No one wants your broken donations.

If it's in great shape but you no longer want it or need it, donate it or sell it in a yard sale or on your local Facebook flea market page.

It's 100% okay to keep things that you love. You *don't* need to throw away something that holds sentimental value to you or brings you happiness. **Just ensure that each item you own has a place.** A place for everything, and everything in its place.

MONDAY
TUESDAY
WEDNESDAY
THURSDAY
FRIDAY
SATURDAY
fn
ctrl

Set Up a Cleaning Schedule

A cleaning schedule is a fantastic way to help keep your house in order. Your home may not always be pristine, but **you'll be amazed by the difference you'll feel in your overall stress** by implementing a simple cleaning schedule.

What is a Cleaning Schedule and Why is it Helpful?

Much like decluttering your home, it's better to do a little at a time than all of it in one day.

Do you want to avoid frantically cleaning your house when guests are coming over? Are you tired of trying to clean your house after it has hit total disaster mode?

If you answered yes, then a cleaning schedule can help.

Certain household chores need to be done each day. You can't wash your dishes once a week and you'll have a big mess if the kids' toys aren't picked up regularly. For other things, you can allocate a day for each task.

How Do You Make a Cleaning Schedule?

If you want a dedicated cleaning schedule, you can find them on Pinterest, or you can create a custom one for yourself.

To create a schedule, **determine what things need to be done daily, weekly, monthly, and yearly.**

You can decide what works best for you and your family, but here's a cheat list for you to base your personalized schedule on.

Daily Tasks

- Wash dishes
- Clean up spills when they happen
- Wipe down kitchen counters
- Sweep high traffic areas
- Pick up toys (or other things out of place)
- Take out garbage (as needed)

- Make the beds

Do a load of laundry (or have a dedicated

-

laundry day)

Organize mail

- **Weekly Tasks**

- Dusting
- Clean bathrooms
- Laundry (unless you choose to do a little each day)

Errands (like grocery shopping)

-

Wash bedsheets

-

Mop and vacuum

-

Kitchen deep clean (including cleaning out

-

old food from the refrigerator) Cut the grass

- Pay bills

- **Monthly Tasks**

- Check smoke alarms
- Dust hard to reach places like ceiling fans
- Knock down cobwebs
- Organize kitchen cabinets
- Wash your bedding (like comforters and duvets)

Wipe down inside and outside of the

-

refrigerator

Deep clean bathrooms -

Wash toys (when applicable) -

Wipe down windows (as needed)

-

Yearly or Seasonal Tasks

Clean out closets (pass on clothes you don't
●

wear, or kids have outgrown)
Wash pillows and stuffed animals
●

Vacuum mattresses ●
Clear outside gutters
●

Move furniture and clean under it
●

Once you've assessed how often you want to do each task, assign a day for them. For example, Mondays are for bathrooms, Tuesdays are for cutting the grass, Wednesdays are for dusting and washing sheets, and so on.

For monthly and yearly tasks, write them on the calendar in big bold letters so you can remember to do them later.

Many busy mothers outsource some of their work. You may want to consider hiring someone to tackle the cleaning tasks. It doesn't make you any less of a mom to do this. You have a lot to oversee and hiring someone to help keep up with the chores is sometimes a necessity.

Another thing you can do is **get the whole family involved in chore duties!** Your kids from little ones on up can help keep things tidy and organized. We'll discuss this more in a later chapter entitled
"Cleaning and Organizing with Kids."

Meal Planning and Meal Prep

Six o'clock rolls around and everyone is looking at you. What's for dinner? You realize that you've gone the whole day with no plans for dinner.

Do you get take-out again this week? (But what about your budget?) Or do you grab a frozen pizza from the freezer even though you wanted something healthier for dinner?

If organizing meals for your week is a struggle with your busy schedule, meal planning and meal prep might be the answer for you.

What is Meal Planning?

Meal planning may sound overwhelming at first. It may even sound constricting. What if you don't *want* lasagna on Wednesday night, right?

Once you give it a chance, though, you'll find that the opposite is true. **It's actually really freeing.** You don't have to wonder if you have enough groceries to last until your next grocery trip, and you won't find yourself at three in the afternoon panicked because you forgot to think about dinner.

If you decide you would rather have tacos on Wednesday, it's no big deal to swap days. If you like to stick to a strict schedule—you've got that covered too.

Setting up a meal plan saves time and money AND takes the burden off thinking "what will we eat today?"

How Do You Make a Meal Plan?

Making a meal plan is fairly simple—and it is entirely relative to how many people you're feeding, what you like to eat, and how many meals you're planning.

Some people plan each meal for the week, including breakfast, lunch, dinner, and snacks. Some people choose to only plan dinners. How you decide this based on your needs.

You may have a cereal-and-granola-barbreakfast- family, or you may think it's important to have

healthier, more involved breakfasts. **Again, how you do your meal planning is largely based on your needs and preferences.**

Plan the Meals

Once you decide how many meals you want to make, it's time to sit down and plan. There are quite a few free and paid meal planning charts available on the internet. You can use those, or you can make your own.

To do this, you just need to write down each day of the week and include whatever mealtimes you're planning for.

Try to choose meals that you know your family enjoys and are not overly difficult to make. You can always toss in a few new recipes each week, but sticking to recipes you're already familiar with makes it much easier when mealtime rolls around.

Another thing to consider is how often you plan on grocery shopping. Some people shop for groceries several times a week, while others shop several times a month.

If you only go every few weeks, remember to use up your fresh produce early before it goes bad.

Create a Grocery List and Go Shopping

When you've finalized your meals, it's time to make a grocery shopping list that matches. Your grocery list should have every item that you need to create the meals you've planned.

What is Meal Prep?

What exactly is meal prep? That's a good question - and not everyone defines it the same way.

Some meal preppers make all of their meals at the beginning of the week and store them in their fridges and freezers to use for the rest of the week.

Others prep individual ingredients that can be used to make meals for the rest of the week.

A third group does a mix of prepared meals and prepped ingredients.

This is another preference-based decision. **There are no wrong answers here.**

The main goal of meal prep is to make things easier for yourself for the remainder of the week. It saves time and energy, and it also alleviates mental stress throughout the week.

Meal planning and meal prep go hand-in-hand, so when you're planning your meals think about ways you can prep them as well.

How Do You Meal Prep?

You can do meal prep in a number of ways. Pick the one that works best for you.
Here are a few methods you can try:

- Prep Individual
- Ingredients Batch Meals
- Freezer Meals
- Snacks
- Premade Meals

Individual Ingredients to Prep

You may not want to create all your meals at the beginning of the week, but there are plenty of short cuts you can do to help make mealtimes easier.
Here are some ideas:

- Clean and chop vegetables early in the ● week. Clean and store fruit.

- Cut chicken into the size and portions you want and freeze or refrigerate.

  Boil eggs and store in the refrigerator.

-
- Cook and store grains and pasta.
- Make yogurt parfaits with fruit or granola.
- Spiralize veggies for pasta alternatives.
- Roast vegetables.
- Make dressings, marinades, and dips.

Batch Meals

Some people choose to cook something at the beginning of the week that they can continue eating throughout the week (or can store in the freezer).
Some examples are:

- Soups
- Stews
- Protein in the crockpot or instant pot
- Legumes
- Salads
- Chili ● Bread

Freezer Meals

Another option is to prep ingredients and freeze raw ingredients to be cooked later.

This often includes:

- Crockpot meals
- Instant pot meals
- Protein in marinades ● Casseroles or Lasagna

Fully Prepared Meals

Another option is creating full meals at the beginning of the week that are completely cooked. These could include freezer meals or meals that are stored in the fridge and just need a reheat.

Usually, this method means that you cook one thing for each meal.

This could include:

- Steel-cut oats
- Breakfast sandwiches
- Rice, protein, veggie bowls
- Stir fry
- Protein, veggie, carbohydrate (of choice)

Snacks That are Easy to Prep Ahead of Time

If you want easy and healthy snacks that you can prepare early in the week, here are some ideas:

- Homemade granola bars
- Cut-up fruit

- Cut-up vegetables
- Sweet potato chips
- Hummus and cut vegetables
- Cut-up cheese and vegetables
- Healthy muffins
- Roasted chickpeas
- Homemade trail mix
- Hardboiled eggs

Food Subscription Boxes

Another option you could consider are food subscription boxes.
Examples:

- HelloFresh
- Freshly
- Marley Spoon
- Dinnerly
- Blue Apron
- Veestro

These subscription box companies send you fresh ingredients ready for you to prepare right at home. You don't have to leave your house or spend hours prepping ingredients. It's all comes ready for you in a box.

It's a more costly option than preparing it all yourself, but it may be something you would like to add to your rotation to take the burden off.

When it comes to meal prep, always keep in mind food storage safety. The FDA has guidelines[1] for

food storage safety and how long individual items can be stored in the refrigerator or freezer.

---

1.   https://www.fda.gov/media/74435/download

Cleaning and Organization with Kids

As a mom, you know how difficult it can be to keep the house organized and clean with kids. Kids are unorganized, on the move, and love to make messes. **One of the best ways to keep the house organized is to get the kids involved with the cleaning and organizing process.**

Even very small children can be included in cleaning and putting things away. You can begin training them when they're very little to be mindful of their toys and to put away something before getting something new out.

Simple Tips to Help Kids Stay Organized

Here are some easy hacks to help keep kids organized and keep your house from total chaos:

1.**A place for everything.** Help kids keep their belongings organized with places to return their things easily—bins, drawers, and more.

You can include pictures or words on the front of bins so they know exactly what belongs there.

2.**Organize their school belongings.** When kids get home from school, they have a

tendency to throw their things everywhere.

Have a plan for when they get home

●

from school. Have a designated place for their coats, shoes, and backpacks.

If they're younger, help them go

•

through their backpacks each day to sort their paperwork. Some papers will have to be completed, some papers may be saved, and some will be thrown away.

If they take a lunch to school, ask

•

them to unpack it so it can be ready

for the next day. Depending on age, you may feel comfortable letting them pack their own lunches. Have them do this as soon as they get home, so it's ready for the next day.

3.Help them declutter their own belongings.

Another thing you can do to help kids get organized is to teach them to declutter their own belongings. Help them understand that they don't have to keep toys that are broken

or that they no longer use or want.

Help them go through clothes that

•

are too small or are in poor shape.

Doing this will help them learn to

•

keep their spaces tidy and cleared of unusable junk.

Age-Appropriate Chores

Teaching your kids to help around the house allows them to learn responsibility and lets them know that they are part of the community of your home.

They're not only capable of helping out, but it also teaches them lifelong skills, like contributing to a group and thinking about the needs of others. It also helps them develop a work ethic.

Here are some chores that your kids can help with based on your child's age and ability. **This is not an extensive list but a sampling of things that children might be able to help with.**

Children Ages 2-3

When your children are very small, the primary goal is to teach them the idea of helping. You're obviously not relying on them to clean the whole house, but they can do their part. You will spend a lot more time guiding them during this stage, but the long-term payoff is big.

Help them to start learning about organizing with chores such as these:

- Pick up toys and put them in bins or designated areas
- Put laundry in the hamper
- Wipe up spills
- Help load washer and dryer
- Wipe walls and baseboards with a wet cloth (they'll probably think this is fun)

Children Ages 4-5

Children of this age will still need more hands-on guidance than they will when they're bigger. They can work more independently than they could at a younger age, but you'll still want to help guide them.

Try these tasks:

- Put away belongings

- Help with laundry
- Carry and put away groceries
- Set the table ● Help clear the table

Children Ages 6-8

You'll probably be amazed at what your kids can do at this age. Children at this age are growing so rapidly emotionally, physically, and mentally. Of course, they're capable of all the things mentioned above, plus a lot more.

Here are some things they're probably able to help with at this age:

- Help care for pets
- Fold and put away laundry
- Vacuum
- Match socks
- Wipe down counters and sinks

Children Ages 9-12

Again, your kids are developing like crazy at this age and becoming more and more independent.

They can help with so many things including:

- Help wash the car
- Learn to wash dishes or load and unload the dishwasher
Rake leaves
-

Learn to wash laundry/switch loads

-

Take care of pets
-

Children (Young Adults) Ages 13-18

Again, you may be surprised by how much children this age are capable of. As they age, they should be able to contribute in many of the same ways that adults would.

Here are some ideas of things they can do in this age range:

- Do the laundry
- Wash the dishes
- Take out the trash
- Help prepare meals
- Clean windows
- Clean bathrooms

- Mop the floor
- Sweep the floor
- Help with many outdoor chores

If you didn't start teaching your kids to help out when they were little, you haven't missed the boat. **You can begin teaching your kids to help out at any age!**

Another important note—avoid feeling discouraged if your kids don't seem capable of doing some of the things on this list at any particular age.

This is a basic guideline and does not account for many variables. Kids develop differently and not all are able to do the same things at the same age.

The main goal is to have them helping in the ways that they can.

Digital Organization

When you think about organization, you may not first think about your digital presence. But researchers are now considering digital clutter as a stressor. Not only that, but all that digital clutter makes your digital devices run more slowly. You've probably experienced the time when your phone or desktop alerts you that you have *no more room*. You missed the perfect photo of your little one because there was no more space on your phone!

In a TEDx Talk called "From Clutter to Clarity," professional organizer Kerry Thomas says,

Digital clutter are things like the ten, twenty, fifty, eighty thousand emails in inboxes that I see on a very regular basis. It's also things like files saved on your computer without naming conventions, so you don't know what you have, and you spend a lot of time looking for things.

Cleaning up your digital devices can help make your life more organized and functional.

Major Areas that Become Disorganized

- Hundreds or thousands of emails (many unopened)
- Messy desktops (loads of files and pictures right on the desktop)
- Hundreds or thousands of unfiled pictures on smartphones
- Unfiled documents on the desktop

- Unemptied download file
- Desktop and smartphone trash bin
- Google Drive Storage
-

How to Declutter Your Digital Spaces

While there are many ways you can clean up your desktop or computer that require a more tech-savvy user, here **the focus is easy and practical things you can do to declutter right away.** You don't need to be a brilliant tech-person or download any special software to complete these tasks.

The Dreaded Inbox

Maybe you delete emails immediately, but many people simply do not. Their inbox is overrun by ads, social media alerts, ten-year-old-emails, and many more.

If you're the type of person who has 10,000 email alerts on their phone, here's how you can get that under control:

1. **Unsubscribe.** There are some emails that you probably love getting or are very important - alerts or newsletters from favorite blogs, messages from friends and

family, emails from your kids' school, or work emails. These emails are why you have an

inbox in the first place.

What you probably don't love getting

-

are multiple ads a day from retailers. Even if you love the retailer and love hearing about their sales, their emails can become aggressive and overwhelming. Unless they're your favorite store in the world, it may be helpful to hit the

"unsubscribe" button.

The same can be true for social

●

media updates. While they can be helpful at times, these emails often tell you things that aren't very useful. You really don't need to know that your second cousin liked a photo, right?

2. **File or Delete.** What should you do with your remaining emails? If you've already read them, you have two choices. You can delete them from your inbox, or you can file them into a specific category.

If you're dealing with work emails,

●

you may want to create separate categories, so you don't delete important documents.

The same is true for emails that you

●

want to keep for sentimental reasons. Create a folder and keep them separate from your main inbox.

SILENCE
IS GOLDEN

For emails that have served their

●

purpose, put them in the trash and move on with your life.

Pictures

Pictures take up a LOT of space on your phones and hard drives. They're one of the most valuable things in your digital possession, but they're also often disorganized and redundant.

Here's how you can help minimize the monster load of pictures you may have:

1.**Delete multiples**. You want the perfect shot, so you took the same photo 10 times. Pick the best one and delete the rest.

2.**Delete the pictures you don't like.** Chances are you have pictures that are blurry, awkward, or ugly. The only reason you still

have them is that you haven't filtered through

your photos in a while. Go ahead and delete all of these.

3.**Delete the pictures you don't care about.**

Yes, that meal you created last Wednesday

was Pinterest-ready. But you really don't

need thirty-five shots of it. (Or maybe any of

it?) Consider if these pictures are still relevant to you. Delete the ones that aren't.

Once you've deleted all the photos you don't want or need from your digital devices, put the one you want to keep on your desktop inside relevant folders. Too many photos in a giant folder are nearly impossible to search, so create unique spaces for them.

You may want to invest in an external hard drive or purchase cloud space for your photos. Just remember to delete the unnecessary photos before you dump them into these spaces.

Folders that Require Regular Cleaning

Here are a few *really* easy ways to clean up your computer or mobile device:

1.**Clear out your downloads.** After a few years, you'll be amazed by how many digital files are living in your Downloads folder. You've downloaded lots of files and instead of finding the proper home, they stay right where they first dropped. Take a day to go through these files.

Most of them can probably be

-

deleted, but the important ones should be filed into their own files.

2. **Throw out the trash.** You deleted a ton of files but still don't have any room left on your device or laptop? Try checking your trash bin. Usually, the trash will be cleared out automatically over time, but you can speed up the process by manually clearing it out right away.

3.**Clean up that desktop.** Your desktop screen can be a beautiful place with the most gorgeous images. Avoid cluttering it up with

files and screenshots. Sure, you can have a few well-organized files in the corner, but most of your files should have a folder of

their own away from your desktop screen.

4.**Clear your history.** Check out your browser history and you'll be amazed by how much information is stored on your computer. Don't delete your saved passwords, but **do clear out your browsing history, cache, cookies, and download history.**

This clears up space on your devices,

●

and it's also a good step in cybersecurity.

Find Time for Relaxation and Rest

The Power of Doing Nothing

Now that you're more productive and organized, you've come to the sweet chapter.

In order to be a productive person, **you need to rest.** You need time to do things you enjoy. You need time when **you're not cleaning, baking cookies, or helping with homework.**

Certainly, by now you've heard the term *self-care*. It may sound silly to you or you may fully embrace it, but moms need time to recharge and refresh.

Julie Burton, author of *The Self-Care Solution: A Modern Mother's Must-Have Guide to Health and Well-Being*, explains in an interview with *Parents* magazine:

> *The moment you become a mother and commit to caring for your child, set an intention for yourself: I will honor and respect myself by regularly taking care of my needs. This will make me happier and better able to care for my family…As moms, we have an enormous opportunity to set a great example for our children of how to be kind to ourselves, and in turn, how to be kind to others. As the saying goes, we can't pour from an empty cup.*

There are certainly some seasons of motherhood that make it more difficult to rest and relax, but if at all possible, **spend some of your time doing absolutely nothing at all (or something that you really enjoy).**

If this seems like a completely unattainable goal, here are some ways for you to get the rest and relaxation that you need mentally, physically, and emotionally.

Don't Do It All Yourself

Today's moms try to do it all. Many are working fulltime jobs, running to all the practices and afterschool events, helping with the PTA, and still finding time to make dinner each night. It's an extremely difficult task to complete alone.

If you have a partner, work out ways to share the innumerable tasks. Don't feel like they're yours alone. Include the kids as well! They can help in many ways—even at a young age.

Ask grandparents to pitch in if they're able or hire a babysitter to watch the kids for a few hours each week, so you can do something you love. There are times when you might need to be alone, but try to develop a community, because **being a mom is a much easier job when you're not doing it alone.**

Take Breaks During the Day

It's true that you're probably not going to be very productive if you watch TV all day. But if you want to watch it for a little while and take a break, don't feel guilty. Maybe you prefer reading a book or going for a walk, talking to a friend on the phone, or creating something.

As busy as you are, **avoid the temptation to skip these small pleasures.** They're important to your health and well-being.

Decide When You're Done for the Day

Taking care of the kids is non-optional, and if you've spent the whole day at work, you'll probably have to take time to clean and make dinner when you get home.

But you should still pick a time of day when you intentionally sit down and set aside your tasks. Your long list of to-dos will be there tomorrow, but your body and mind need rest.

Choose a quitting time for yourself when you don't have to *do anything else.*

Get Some Rest

Moms don't always get to sleep. They're up at night with infants and toddlers and they're there when their kids don't feel well. But Moms need sleep too.

According to a study by scientist and physician Dr. Jeffery Ellenbogen, "Sleep loss causes profound impairments in cognitive and behavioral performance." In other words, people have trouble performing and being productive when they aren't getting enough sleep.

If your kids sleep through the night, try to create a habit of getting to bed at a reasonable time. Set aside your screens, read a book, and get some shut eye.

If you're often up with a little one during the night, understand that it is a season of your life. Lower your expectations for the number of things you will accomplish. Take naps when you can and ask for plenty of help.

The Final Wrap Up

If you're thinking "I could never be that organized!" **start with one chapter at a time.** Pick the one that appeals to you the most and implement one change. Try your hand at meal planning or work on decluttering one room in your house. Don't feel like you have to accomplish every step in this book or you're a failure.

Changing your habits to become a more productive, more organized person does not happen suddenly. It's a gradual change. As you begin changing small habits, you'll find that you get big dividends. That change will help spur on additional changes and give you the ambition to keep trying.

Once you're able to implement these changes, **you'll be amazed at the results.** Things that once felt like huge obstacles will soon feel like things you can handle.

Because you have habits and systems in place, you won't find yourself struggling to remember your kid's homework. You have a place for that. You'll still have laundry to do, but it'll be managed. You'll still have to put away the toys, but you'll have a place for them.

These easy steps will create *big* changes in your life. Just remember to do it a little at a time and soon you will experience success.

THE PRODUCTIVE MOM -

Title: Nurturing Wholeness: A Guide to Rediscovering Yourself After Parenthood

The journey into parenthood is undoubtedly transformative, marked by moments of immense joy, profound love, and an overwhelming sense of responsibility. As parents embark on this life-altering adventure, they often find themselves navigating uncharted territories, learning the delicate dance of caring for a new life while grappling with the evolving facets of their own identity.

While the joys of parenthood are unparalleled, the challenges it brings can be equally profound, especially when it comes to maintaining a sense of self. The demands of nurturing and providing for a growing family can sometimes overshadow one's individuality, leaving parents to grapple with the question, "Where do I fit into this new version of my life?"

In this exploration of post-parenthood identity, we delve into the common challenges parents face in preserving their sense of self amidst. the beautiful chaos of raising children. From embracing change to carv- ing out moments for self-reflection, this guide aims to illuminate the path toward rediscovering personal wholeness in the midst of the trans- formative journey that is parenthood. Embracing Change: A Vital Step in the Parenthood Odyssey

Parenthood is a journey that reshapes every facet of life. From the moment a child enters the world, the landscape of a parent's existence undergoes a profound transformation. Acknowledging and understand- ing these changes is a crucial first step towards navigating the intricate path of post-parenthood self-discovery.

It's essential to recognize that parenthood introduces a myriad of shifts – in priorities, routines, and even perspectives. The once familiar rhythm of life is now set to the beat of a tiny heartbeat, and this adjust- ment can be both exhilarating and challenging. It involves relinquishing certain aspects of personal freedom and adapting to a new set of responsibilities.

Acceptance of these changes is pivotal. Rather than resisting the shift, viewing it as a natural progression allows parents to approach their new reality with a sense of openness. Acceptance fosters resilience, en- abling individuals to weather the inevitable storms of parenthood with a more balanced and composed demeanor.

Adaptation is the companion to acceptance. It involves the intentional process of aligning oneself with the evolving dynamics of family life. This may require redefining personal goals, adjusting expectations, and finding joy in the small, often overlooked, moments of daily life. As parents adapt to their new roles, they discover strength in flexibility and resilience in the face of unexpected challenges.

In the tapestry of parenthood, embracing change becomes a transfor- mative act of self-discovery. It is an ongoing dialogue with oneself, where the narrative evolves to include the intricacies of being both an individ- ual and a parent. By acknowledging the shifts, accepting the new nor- mal, and adapting with grace, parents can lay a sturdy foundation for the journey toward rediscovering personal wholeness after the arrival of their precious ones

Self-Reflection: Illuminating the Path to Personal Rediscovery

In the whirlwind of parenting, where days seamlessly blend into nights and responsibilities often eclipse individuality, the practice of self- reflection emerges as a beacon guiding parents back to themselves. En- couraging moments of in- trospection can be transformative, offering a space for parents to reconnect with their evolving identity and rediscover the facets of life that bring them genuine joy.

Amidst the chaos of diaper changes and bedtime stories, carving out time for self-reflection might seem like an elusive luxury. However, it is a crucial in- vestment in personal well-being. Taking a deliberate pause allows parents to ask themselves fundamental questions that often get drowned out in the cacophony of parental duties.

"Who am I now?" This question serves as a compass, guiding par

ents through the labyrinth of identity shifts that accompany parenthood. It prompts individuals to acknowledge the changes they've undergone – the amal- gamation of roles as caregivers, mentors, and providers. By re- flecting on this transformation, parents can better understand their pre- sent selves and lay the groundwork for future personal growth.

"What brings me joy?" Amidst the responsibilities, rediscovering joy is essential for maintaining a sense of self. Whether it's a forgotten hobby, a quiet moment with a book, or a simple walk in nature, identify- ing and prioritizing activities that bring genuine happiness is a powerful form of self-care. Reflecting on these sources of joy allows parents to inte- grate them into their daily lives, creating a harmonious balance between nurturing a family and nourishing the individual.

Self-reflection is not a luxury; it is a necessity. It provides the clarity needed to navigate the intricate dance between parenthood and personal identity. By encouraging parents to engage in this introspective journey, we empower them to cultivate a deeper understanding of themselves, fostering a resilient foundation for the ongoing quest to rediscover wholeness in the beautiful chaos of raising children.

.**Prioritizing Self-Care: Nurturing the Caregiver Within**

In the intricate tapestry of parenthood, where every thread is woven with love and dedication, it's easy for parents to inadvertently neglect the weaver—their own well-being. Prioritizing self-care is not a selfish act; it's a fundamental step in maintaining mental and emotional equilibri- um, ensuring that caregivers can provide the best of themselves to their families. Here, we explore the significance of selfcare and offer practical tips for seamlessly integrating it into the demanding routine of parenting.

Stress the Significance of Self-Care:

The demands of parenting can be relentless, and the toll on mental and emotional well-being is often underestimated. Stress, fatigue, and burnout can become unwelcome companions on the parenting journey. Emphasizing the significance of self-care is a recognition that a healthy, fulfilled caregiver is better equipped to navigate the challenges of raising a family.

Self-care is not a luxury but a necessity. It is the intentional act of replenishing one's energy, nurturing the soul, and creating a reservoir of resilience. By acknowledging the importance of self-care, parents empower themselves to break free from the guilt often associated with taking time for personal well-being.

Practical Tips for Integration:

1.**Micro-Moments of Self-Care:** In a bustling household, finding extended periods for self-care can be challenging.

However, embracing micro-moments of self-care can be just as impactful. Whether it's savoring a hot cup of tea, stealing a few

minutes of quiet reflection, or enjoying a short walk, these small acts can accumulate to create a profound sense of wellb eing .

Schedule "Me Time": Treat personal time with the same importance as any other commitment. Schedule dedicated "me time" on the calendar, whether it's a weekly yoga class, a solitary walk, or even a brief escape to read a favorite book. This designated time serves as a non-negotiable appointment with oneself.

Delegate and Share Responsibilities: Parenting is a team effort. Sharing responsibilities with a partner or seeking support from friends and family allows parents the freedom to prioritize self-care without feeling burdened by guilt.

1.**Create a Self-Care Toolkit:** Identify activities that bring joy

and relaxation. Whether it's listening to music, practicing mindfulness, or engaging in a creative pursuit, having a

toolkit
of go-to self-care activities provides quick and accessible options during hectic moments.

1.**Establish Boundaries:** Set clear boundaries between parenting responsibilities and personal time. Communicate these boundaries with family members to create a supportive environment that respects the need for self-care.

PRIORITIZING SELF-CARE is an investment in both personal and familial well-being. By recognizing its importance and incorporating practical strategies into daily life, parents can navigate the challenges of parenting with resilience, fostering a harmonious balance between nur- turing others and caring for the caregiver within.

Communication with Partner: Building Bridges in Parenthood

Parenthood is a shared journey, and the strength of the parental bond often depends on the foundation of open communication. Emphasizing the need for a transparent dialogue with a partner about personal needs and goals becomes crucial in navigating the complex terrain of raising children. Here, we explore the significance of communication and share strategies for fostering a resilient connection amidst the demands of parenting.

Emphasize the Need for Open Communication:

Open communication is the cornerstone of a thriving partnership, especially in the context of parenthood. As roles evolve and responsibil- ities multiply, expressing one's needs, concerns, and aspirations becomes paramount. This open dialogue allows partners to align their expectations, providing a solid framework for mutual support.

Encourage the cultivation of a safe space where both partners feel heard and understood. Acknowledge that each person brings unique per- spectives and challenges to the parenting journey. Embracing open com- munication lays the groundwork for building a partnership that not only survives but thrives in the face of the challenges that parenting presents.

Strategies for Maintaining a Strong Connection:

1.**Scheduled Check-Ins:** Set aside dedicated time for regular check-ins with your partner. These moments allow for a

focused discussion about individual experiences, challenges, and triumphs. Whether it's a weekly coffee date or a quiet evening at home, these check-ins foster connection and reinforce the idea that you are navigating parenthood together.

1.**Shared Goals and Expectations:** Establish shared goals and ex- pectations for both parenting and personal growth.

Understanding each other's aspirations helps create a roadmap for the future and ensures that individual goals complement

rather than compete with each other.

Team Approach to Parenting: Frame parenting as a collaborative effort. Adopting a team mentality reinforces the idea that both partners contribute to the family's well-being. Discuss and delegate responsibilities based on individual strengths and interests, fostering a sense of shared ownership in the parenting journey.

Celebrate Small Wins: Parenting can be a series of small victories and challenges. Celebrate the successes, no matter how minor, together. Acknowledging and appreciating each other's contributions fosters a positive environment and strengthens the emotional connection between partners.

Prioritize Quality Time: Amidst the whirlwind of parenting, prioritize quality time with your partner. Whether it's a weekend getaway, a movie night at home, or a simple dinner, these moments of connection reinforce the foundation of your relationship outside the realm of parenting responsibilities.

OPEN COMMUNICATION is not only about discussing challenges but also about celebrating victories and maintaining a sense of unity. By prioritizing this dialogue and implementing strategies that strengthen the partnership, couples can navigate parenthood with resilience, ensuring that their connection remains a source of strength and support amidst the beautiful chaos of raising children.

Building a Support System: Navigating Parenthood Together
Parenthood is a collective experience, and the significance of a supportive community cannot be overstated. In the intricate dance of raising children, having a network of understanding friends and fellow parents can be a source of strength, shared wisdom, and emotional sustenance. Here, we delve into the importance of a supportive community and explore ways to connect with other parents to build a resilient network.
The Importance of a Supportive Community:

Parenthood is a journey with its peaks and valleys, and having a supportive community can make all the difference. A network of understanding friends and fellow parents provides a sense of belonging, valida- tion, and shared experi- ence. It serves as a reminder that you are not alone

in the challenges and joys of raising children.

A supportive community offers diverse perspectives, insights, and practical advice. Whether it's navigating sleepless nights, discussing de- velopmental milestones, or sharing tips on self-care, the collective wis- dom of a community can be a valuable resource. It becomes a space to lean on during tough times and celebrate together during moments of

triumph.

Ways to Connect and Build a Network:

1.**Parenting Groups:** Join local or online parenting groups where individuals share their experiences, seek advice, and provide support. These groups often organize meet-ups,

creating opportunities to connect in person.

Attend Parenting Classes or Workshops: Participate in parenting classes or workshops in your community. These environments not on- ly offer valuable knowledge but also provide a chance to meet other parents who may share similar challenges and interests.

Utilize Social Media: Engage with parenting communities on so- cial media platforms. Join forums, follow parenting blogs, and partici- pate in discussions. While online connections are virtual, they can still offer a sense of camaraderie and support.

Local Events and Meet-Ups: Attend local events or meetups specifically designed for parents. These gatherings may include playgroups, storytime sessions, or family-friendly activities, creating opportunities to form connections with other parents.

1.**Reach Out to Friends and Family:** Strengthen existing connections with friends who are also parents or family

members who understand the dynamics of parenthood. Foster these relationships by scheduling regular catch-ups or even

organizing joint family activities.

Create a Supportive Circle: Identify individuals who resonate with your parenting style and values. Cultivate deeper

connections with these friends, creating a small circle where you can share openly and offer support to one another.

BUILDING A SUPPORT system is a proactive step in fortifying your journey through parenthood. By recognizing the importance of community, actively seeking connections, and fostering relationships with understanding friends, you create a safety net that enhances not only your well-being but also the richness of your parenting experience.

Pursuing Passions: Nurturing the Flame Beyond Parenthood

Parenthood is a transformative chapter that often prompts individuals to reevaluate priorities. However, the pursuit of personal passions need not be sacrificed on the altar of caregiving responsibilities. Encouraging parents to revisit or discover new passions is not only a form of selfcare but also a pathway to maintaining a sense of individuality. Here, we explore the importance of pursuing passions and share inspiring stories of individuals who have successfully balanced parenthood with personal pursuits.

Encouraging the Rediscovery of Passions:

Parenthood does not mark the end of personal aspirations; rather, it introduces an opportunity to integrate one's passions into the multifaceted tapestry of family life. Encouraging parents to revisit or discover new passions is an investment in personal fulfillment, creativity, and overall well-being.

Reconnecting with a hobby or pursuing a new interest can be a revitalizing experience. It allows parents to tap into aspects of themselves beyond the parental role, fostering a sense of identity that extends beyond the responsibilities of caregiving. Whether it's a long-loved hobby or a newfound interest, passions provide an outlet for self-expression and joy.

Inspiring Stories of Balance:

1.*The Artist-Parent:* Meet Sarah, a mother of two who, amidst the chaos of parenting, rediscovered her love for painting. By dedicating a few hours each week to her art, Sarah not only

found solace and joy but also set an inspiring example for her children, showcasing the importance of pursuing one's passions.

The Fitness Enthusiast: John, a father of three, integrated his passion for fitness into family life. He started family workout sessions, turning exercise into quality time. Not only did this contribute to a healthier lifestyle for the entire family, but it also allowed John to indulge in his passion without compromising family time.

1.*The Bookworm Parent:* Emily, a book lover, transformed her passion into a family affair. She initiated a weekly family reading night, where each member shared their favorite books.

This not only nurtured a love for literature in her children but also allowed Emily to indulge in her passion while fostering family connection.

THESE STORIES ILLUMINATE the possibility of harmonizing personal passions with the demands of parenthood. They showcase that, with intentional planning and a commitment to self-expression, parents can navigate the delicate balance between nurturing a family and nourishing their own passions. By encouraging this pursuit, we empower parents to lead more fulfilled lives, embracing the totality of their identities beyond the role of caregivers.

Building a Support System: Navigating Parenthood Together

Parenthood is a collective experience, and the significance of a supportive community cannot be overstated. In the intricate dance of raising children, having a network of understanding friends and fellow parents can be a source of strength, shared wisdom, and emotional sustenance. Here, we delve into the importance of a supportive community and ex- plore ways to connect with other parents to build a resilient network.

The Importance of a Supportive Community:

Parenthood is a journey with its peaks and valleys, and having a supportive community can make all the difference. A network of understanding friends and fellow parents provides a sense of belonging, valida- tion, and shared experience. It serves as a reminder that you are not alone

in the challenges and joys of raising children.

A supportive community offers diverse perspectives, insights, and practical advice. Whether it's navigating sleepless nights, discussing de- velopmental milestones, or sharing tips on self-care, the collective wis- dom of a community can be a valuable resource. It becomes a space to lean on during tough times and celebrate together during moments of

triumph.

Ways to Connect and Build a Network:

1.**Parenting Groups:** Join local or online parenting groups where individuals share their experiences, seek advice, and provide support. These groups often organize meet-ups,

creating opportunities to connect in person.

Attend Parenting Classes or Workshops: Participate in parenting classes or workshops in your community. These environments not only offer valuable knowledge but also provide a chance to meet other parents who may share similar challenges and interests.

Utilize Social Media: Engage with parenting communities

on social media platforms. Join forums, follow parenting blogs, and participate in discussions. While online connections are virtual, they can still offer a sense of camaraderie and support.

Local Events and Meet-Ups: Attend local events or meetups specifically designed for parents. These gatherings may include playgroups, storytime sessions, or family-friendly activities, creating opportunities to form connections with other parents.

1. **Reach Out to Friends and Family:** Strengthen existing connections with friends who are also parents or family members who understand the dynamics of parenthood. Foster these relationships by scheduling regular catch-ups or even

organizing joint family activities.

1. **Create a Supportive Circle:** Identify individuals who resonate with your parenting style and values. Cultivate deeper connections with these friends, creating a small circle where you can share openly and offer support to one another.

BUILDING A SUPPORT system is a proactive step in fortifying your journey through parenthood. By recognizing the importance of community, actively seeking connections, and fostering relationships with understanding friends, you create a safety net that enhances not only your well-being but also the richness of your parenting experience.

Mindfulness and Presence: Anchoring Amidst Parenting Chaos

In the whirlwind of parenting, where every moment seems to demand attention, the practice of mindfulness emerges as a transformative tool. Mindfulness, the art of being present in the current moment with- out judgment, offers parents a sanctuary amidst the chaos. Here, we in- troduce mindfulness as a means

of

staying grounded and provide simple

exercises for parents to seamlessly incorporate into their daily lives.
Introducing Mindfulness as a Tool:
Mindfulness is more than a trendy concept; it is a powerful tool for cultivating presence and awareness in the midst of life's busyness. For parents, it offers a respite from the constant juggling of responsibilities, providing a moment of clarity and calm in the storm of parenting chaos. The essence of mindfulness lies in"the intentional focus on the present moment, acknowledging thoughts and sensations without becom- ing overwhelmed by them. This practice not only nurtures emotional well-being but also enhances the quality of interactions with children, fostering deeper connections and understanding. **Simple Mindfulness Exercises for Parents:**

1.**Breath Awareness:** Take a few minutes each day to focus on your breath. Find a quiet space, sit comfortably, and pay attention to the sensation of your breath as you inhale and exhale. This simple exercise grounds you in the present

moment and can be done anytime, anywhere.

Mindful Observation: Engage in mindful observation during routine activities. Whether it's savoring the aroma of a cup of coffee or fully experiencing the warmth of sunlight during a family walk, bring your attention to the sensory details of the moment.

Body Scan: Conduct a brief body scan to check in with yourself. Starting from your toes and moving up to the top of your head, notice any tension or sensations. This practice enhances body awareness and can be particularly beneficial during moments of stress.

Mindful Listening: Practice mindful listening during interactions with your children. Put aside distractions, make eye contact, and truly listen to what they are saying. This fosters a deeper connection and enriches the quality of communication.

1.**Gratitude Journaling:** Dedicate a few minutes each day to jot down things you are grateful for. This simple practice shifts focus to positive aspects of life, fostering a mindset of appreciation amidst the challenges of parenting.

INCORPORATING THESE mindfulness exercises into daily life doesn't require significant time commitments. Instead, they serve assubtle yet potent reminders to anchor oneself in the present moment. By embracing mindfulness, parents can navigate the complexities ofparenthood with a heightened sense of awareness, fostering resilience and a deeper connection with both themselves and their children.

Professional Development and Learning: Nurturing Growth Beyond Parenthood

Parenthood is a transformative journey, and while it brings a multitude of responsibilities, it doesn't signal the end of personal and professional aspirations. In fact, the period after having children can be a

pow-

erful time for pursuing new career paths or educational goals. Let's explore the possibility of professional development and learning

post-par- enthood, highlighting inspiring examples of parents who have success- ful- ly navigated career changes or educational pursuits.

Pursuing Professional or Educational Goals After Parenthood:

The decision to pursue professional or educational goals after having children is a personal one, shaped by individual

aspirations and circum- stances. Contrary to the notion that parenthood limits career growth, it

can serve as a catalyst for self-discovery and empowerment. The post-parenthood phase offers an opportunity for reflection. Par-

ents often reassess their values, skills, and long-term goals,

leading to a renewed sense of purpose. Whether it's a desire for career advancement, a passion for a different field, or a

commitment to lifelong learning, the journey of professional development after parenthood is diverse and uniquely tailored to each individual.

Examples of Successful Navigations:

1.**Career Switch Success:** Meet Lisa, a mother of two, who, after having children, decided to switch careers from finance to counseling. Through part-time education, internships, and a
supportive network, she successfully transitioned, combining her love for helping others with her professional skills.

Entrepreneurial Ventures: John, a father of three, embraced entrepreneurship after becoming a parent. Recognizing the need for flexible hours, he founded a successful consulting business that allowed him to balance his career ambitions with active participation in his children's lives.

Academic Achievements: Sarah, a mother with a passion

for literature, pursued a master's degree in English literature after her children started school. Balancing studies with parenting, she not only achieved academic success but also instilled a love for learning in her children.

1.**Skill Enhancement:** James, a father of twins, focused on skill enhancement after becoming a parent. Through online courses and workshops, he developed expertise in digital marketing, opening up new opportunities for career growth while maintaining a flexible schedule.

THESE EXAMPLES ILLUSTRATE that the post-parenthood phase can be a time of empowerment and growth. With determination, strategic planning, and a supportive environment, parents can successfully navigate career changes or educational pursuits, enriching their lives and serving as inspiring role models for their children.

In embracing the possibility of professional development and learning after parenthood, individuals not only invest in their own growth but also contribute to a broader narrative that challenges societal expectations and celebrates the multifaceted nature of modern parenting

Conclusion: Nurturing Wholeness in the Parenthood Journey

In the intricate dance of parenthood, where love intertwines with challenges, the quest for personal wholeness emerges as a transformative journey. From embracing change to setting boundaries, from pursuing passions to professional growth, each step contributes to the ongoing process of rediscovering oneself after having children. Key Points:

1.**Embracing Change:** Acknowledge the transformative nature of parenthood, recognizing that change is a constant

companion on this journey. Acceptance and adaptation lay the

foundation for a balanced approach to the new roles and responsibilities that accompany raising children.

Self-Reflection: Encourage parents to embark on a journey of self-discovery by asking fundamental questions about their evolving identity. The process of self-reflection serves as a compass, guiding individuals towards a deeper understanding of who they are amidst the beautiful chaos of parenting.

1.**Prioritizing Self-Care:** Stress the significance of self-care as a non-negotiable aspect of maintaining mental and emotional well-being. Practical tips empower parents to integrate self-care

seamlessly into their busy routines, ensuring they have the resilience to navigate the challenges of parenthood.

Communication with Partner: Emphasize the importance of open communication with a partner about personal needs and goals. Strategies for maintaining a strong connection reinforce the idea that a supportive partnership is a cornerstone in the journey to wholeness.

1.**Building a Support System:** Discuss the crucial role of a supportive community in providing understanding and shared

wisdom. Exploring ways to connect with other parents emphasizes that the journey is not meant to be walked alone. **Pursuing Passions:** Encourage the rediscovery or exploration of personal passions, showcasing that parenthood need not stifle individual aspirations. Inspiring stories illustrate that passions can be integrated into the fabric of family life, enriching both the individual and the family unit.

Setting Boundaries: Explore the concept of setting healthy boundaries to balance responsibilities without sacrificing personal well-being. Guidance on effective time management and communication empowers parents to navigate the delicate equilibrium of caregiving and self-care.

Mindfulness and Presence: Introduce mindfulness as a transformative tool for staying present amidst parenting chaos. Simple exercises offer practical ways for parents to incorporate mindfulness into their daily lives, fostering awareness and resilience.

1.**Professional Development and Learning:** Discuss the possibility of pursuing professional or educational goals after having children. Examples of successful navigations illustrate

that the post-parenthood phase can be a time of empowerment, growth, and the pursuit of new horizons.

REINFORCING THE IDEAof Ongoing Process:

Finding wholeness after having kids is not a destination but a contin- uous journey. Each step, whether big or small, contributes to the evolv- ing narrative of personal growth and fulfillment. Parenthood, far from limiting individuality, becomes a catalyst for self-discovery and empowerment.

Encouragement to Be Patient and Celebrate Small Victories:

In this journey, patience is a virtue. The road to wholeness is marked by progress, not perfection. Parents are urged to be patient with them- selves, acknowledging that self-discovery is a gradual process. Celebrate the small victories, relish in the moments of joy, and recognize that every step taken towards personal fulfillment is a triumph worth celebrating.

As parents navigate the beautiful chaos of raising children, may they find solace in the unfolding journey of self-discovery, embracing the to- tality of their identity, and cultivating a sense of wholeness that extends beyond the roles of caregiver.

About Arthur

Meet Penny, a practical and devoted mom and grandmother who seamlessly juggles her roles as a family-oriented matriarch and a life coach. With a keen focus on helping women utilize their time wisely, Penny dedicates herself to coaching others towards a less stressful and more functional life. Her commitment extends beyond her immediate family, as she empowers women through coaching, imparting valuable skills for a balanced and fulfilling lifestyle. Penny's journey embodies a harmonious blend of practicality, family dedication, and a passion for nurturing the well-being of those around her.

Don't miss out!

Visit the website below and you can sign up to receive emails whenever Penny White publishes a new book. There's no charge and no obligation.

https://books2read.com/r/B-A-UIQBB-SDFRC

BOOKS 2 READ

Connecting independent readers to independent writers.

About the Publisher

Meet Penny, a practical and devoted mom and grandmother who seamlessly juggles her roles as a family-oriented matriarch and a life coach. With a keen focus on helping women utilize their time wisely, Penny dedicates herself to coaching others towards a less stressful and more functional life. Her commitment extends beyond her immediate family, as she empowers women through coaching, imparting valuable skills for a balanced and fulfilling lifestyle. Penny's journey embodies a harmonious blend of practicality, family dedication, and a passion for nurturing the well-being of those around her.

Read more at https://lifesajourneyllc.godaddysites.com/.